# Christmas

DEC **25**

MERRY CHRISTMAS!

## Dorothy Goeller

**Bailey Books**
an imprint of
**Enslow Publishers, Inc.**

Bailey Books, an imprint of Enslow Publishers, Inc.

**Library of Congress Cataloging-in-Publication Data**

Goeller, Dorothy.
Christmas / Dorothy Goeller.
p. cm. — (All about holidays)
   Includes index.
Summary: "Simple text and photographs present a story with a Christmas theme"
—Provided
by publisher.
ISBN 978-0-7660-3805-9
1. Christmas—Juvenile literature. I. Title.
GT4985.5.G64 2011
394.2663—dc22

                              2010013460
Paperback ISBN: 978-1-59845-174-0

Printed in the United States of America

062010 Lake Book Manufacturing, Inc., Melrose Park, IL

10 9 8 7 6 5 4 3 2 1

**Photo Credits:** Shutterstock.com

**Cover Photo:** Shutterstock.com

# Note to Parents and Teachers

Help pre-readers get a jumpstart on reading. These lively stories introduce simple concepts
with repetition of words and short simple sentences. Photos and illustrations fill the pages
with color and effectively enhance the text. Free Educator Guides are available for this
series at www.enslow.com. Search for the *All About Holidays* series name.

# Contents

# Words to Know

**fish**       **Santa**       **stars**

# DEAR SANTA

For Christmas,
I want a tree,

A tree and lots of stars,

A tree and lots of stars, and candy canes.

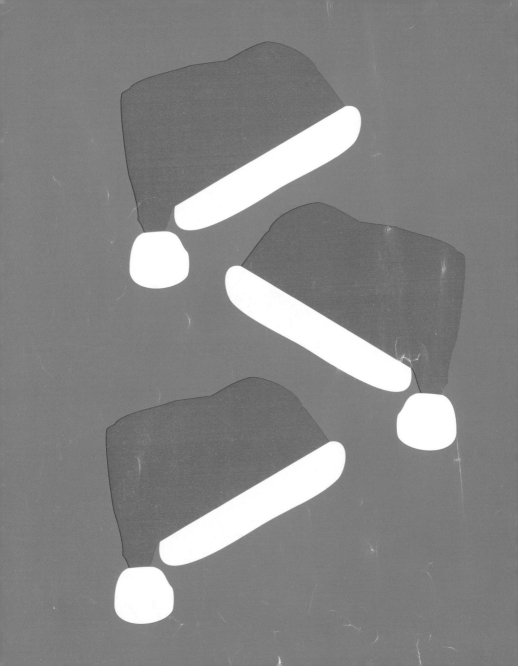

A tree and lots of stars, and candy canes, and hats.

A tree and lots of stars, and candy canes, and hats, and fish!

# Fish?

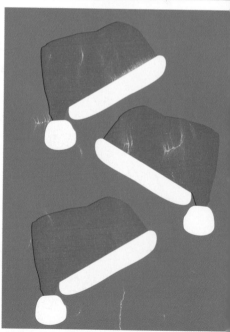

Yes, a tree and lots
of stars, and candy
canes, and hats,
and fish!

# Fish are the best gift of all!

Thanks, Santa!

# Read More

Rey, H.A. *Merry Christmas, Curious George!* New York: Houghton Mifflin, 2006.

Wells, Rosemary. *Max's Christmas.* New York: Viking Juvenile, 2010.

# Web Sites

Preschool Education Arts & Crafts. *Holidays—Christmas.* <http://www.preschooleducation.com/achristmas.shtml>

DLTK's Holiday Activities for Kids: *Christmas Activities.* <http://www.dltk-holidays.com/xmas/index.html>

# Index

Guided Reading Level: **B**
Guided Reading Leveling System is based on the guidelines recommended by Fountas and Pinnell.

Word Count: 71

ma

5

11